SPIRITUAL WARFARE!

Turning the Tide

with

Rivers of the Heart

MARY DONNA HANKLA

Book Cover by Sermonassist

Illustrations by Katerina R

1st edition 2023

ISBN: 979-8-9880394-2-6

Library of Congress Control Number: 2023924375

KJV – King James Version. Scripture quotations marked in "KJV" are taken from the Holy Bible, King James Version, Cambridge, 1769

AMP – The Amplified Study Bible. Scripture quotations marked in "AMP" are taken from the Amplified Study Bible, Copyright © 2017 by Zondervan, Grand Rapids, MI 49496.

DEDICATION

This is the second book that I have written. It brings me immense joy to share the wonderful things that God has done for me and my family.

I express my deepest appreciation to my husband and son, Kenny and Chris Hankla, who have provided invaluable support. Chris, skilled in computer technology, dedicated countless hours to the technical aspects of the book.

Additionally, I dedicate this book to the Big 4 P.H. Church in Kimball, WV. For over fifteen years, our family has pastored this church. The elders of the church are truly people of faith and exceptional prayer warriors. Cecil and Brenda have provided much encouragement.

Finally, this book is dedicated to the Appalachian Conference located in Dublin, Virginia. Bishop Preston Mathena and the conference board serve the Lord with great zeal, offering ample support and prayers. Pastor Debbie Hutton and her husband, Butch, are wonderful friends who have stood by me for many years. Together, we have worked as WIN prayer leaders, conducting prayer incentives for our nation, churches, the conference, pastors, and others. We teach about prayer on YouTube and Facebook. Debbie and Butch pastor the Faith Temple Church in Pearisburg, VA.

Pastor Stacy Cope, who encouraged me to write a book, is an inspiration to ministers. He always wears a smile and has a deep desire to help people break free from various forms of bondage. He and his wife, Sunny, a woman of great faith, both pastor the Tower of Refuge Church in Dublin, VA.

CONTENTS

FOREWORD

To say that Mary "Donna" Hankla is a friend is a privilege. To say she is a unique, godly woman of prayer and commitment is a gross understatement. I have known her for twenty-plus years. When I first met her, I recognized her as a woman with an authentic and exceptional passion for Jesus and His Word. It was and is her first priority in life, and prayer is her lifeline.

Soon after meeting Donna, I knew I wanted to have her speak on prayer at my church, where I served as an associate pastor. I remember saying truthfully that I would rather listen to her speak and teach on prayer and Christian living than Joyce Meyer or many others I listen to and am blessed by. Donna Hankla, my friend, is the real deal!

She has a unique writing style, using short sentences that are to the point. Without being verbose, her words, born from vast knowledge and application of the Word, and how it has enriched her life, will challenge and bless yours. The words she shares in this book are like arrows hitting a target and landing on the bullseye every time!

This power-packed book will bless all readers, whether they are new Christians or seasoned followers of Jesus of all ages and maturity levels. Donna combines truths that are essential elements of prayer and Scripture.

From her life experiences, she speaks words of wisdom that will enrich your life. You will want to read *SPIRITUAL WARFARE! TURNING THE TIDE WITH RIVERS OF THE*

HEART again and again.

Debbie Hutton
Senior Pastor Faith Temple
IPHC Assistant Director
WIN (World Intercessors Network) Appalachian Conference

I don't find it by chance or coincidence that it is pouring down rain outside my office and home as I prepare to write this foreword for Rev. Donna Hankla. The heavens are opening up and pouring down fresh waters of life onto the earth so that God's creation can continue to be fed and grow. Any reader who takes the time to read her marvelous creation will be refreshed, renewed, and replenished. I don't know about you, but in this world we are living in, I need refreshing daily—physically, mentally, spiritually, and as a pastor, I must say, socially.

In our generation, we have the honor and privilege of showering or bathing daily, and for those like me who don't like to feel dirty or dingy, sometimes twice a day. Going back only a couple of generations, most common people didn't have the luxury of bathing daily as we do today. We have become adaptive to this physical luxury and take advantage of it. We also have the luxury of having the Bible and many great books written by wonderful authors at our fingertips on our smartphones, iPads, and computers.

If I had the power to persuade anyone to take the time to read this book, I would. Donna has a wonderful way of keeping the reader captivated from one chapter and story to the next, and I didn't want to put the book down. She shares her real-life testimonies in each chapter; I could feel myself right beside her in the midst of the story, and that gave me strength and courage to face some of my own life struggles and challenges I've been facing lately.

Honestly, when I read the "Rivers of Joy" part in the book, I started to cry and pray for God's joy to flow over me and renew my joy again. Sometimes unexpected surprises come our way, and if we are not careful, our joy can be stolen by the enemy. Donna quotes from the Bible that Satan is a thief, and he wants to steal, kill, and destroy, but Jesus came to give life and give it more abundantly (John 10:10).

If you need some more of Jesus and the more abundant life that He gives, read this book and be filled with the love of the Father, grace of the Son, and comfort of His Spirit. I believe rivers of love, grace, and comfort will flow into your heart!

Pastor Stacy C. Cope
Pastor & Author
Lead Pastor of Tower of Refuge Church
www.testimoniestold.com

INTRODUCTION

When rivers from the heart begin to flow, buried dreams are resurrected. Disappointments are washed away, and seeds of hope spring forth. Living waters sprout those seeds that lay dormant in the ground!

Even as underground springs release water to the surrounding areas, the heart spews out streams of life. If the heart is guided by the Holy Spirit, refreshing waters will flow!

"Watch over your heart with all diligence, For from it flow the springs of life" (Proverbs 4:23 Amplified Version).

TOUCHED BY THE WATERS

There were times in my life when I needed living waters to pour over me. Like so many others, I experienced moments of trauma, disappointment, and uncertainty.

I prayed for rivers of God's grace to flow into my heart, and I was not disappointed. A powerful lesson was learned: disappointments did not have to rule my life. I found a scripture, a living stream of hope, to pray.

"Such hope (in God's promises) never disappoints us, because God's love has been abundantly poured out within our hearts through the Holy Spirit who was given to us" (Romans 5:5 Amplified Version)

Insomnia nearly derailed my first semester in college. I needed those rivers of living water to heal my soul! I encountered these waters when I went to the chapel for prayer. As the minister prayed for me, I felt God's peace wash over my soul!

That very night, sleep came with ease. I had barely laid my head on the pillow before I fell asleep. And ever since that moment, sleep has not been an issue!

AN INVITATION

"Everyone who thirsts come to the waters; And you who have no money come; buy grain and eat. Come, buy wine and milk - Without money and without cost (simply accept it as a gift from God) (Isaiah 55:1 Amplified Version).

If you are hurting, come to the waters!

If you are thirsty (in need), come to the waters!

If you are weary, come to the waters!

Allow those living waters of grace to wash away bitterness, disappointments, and failures.

RECEIVE

Three things are promised to those who come to the waters.

1. Water of Life
   The water of life will quench the thirst of the soul! For those who have been through dry and difficult times, living waters will bring refreshing.

2. Milk for Strength and Nourishment
   Milk for strength and nourishment is provided. These waters will strengthen the weak and weary.

3. Wine for Joy

Wine for joy will bring gladness. This is not the wine for being drunk. For those who have forgotten to laugh, these waters will bring encouragement.

New wine symbolizes a release of God's Holy Spirit. Jesus associated new wine with the harvest (Matthew 9:17).

CHAPTER 1

SEEDS OF ETERNITY PLANTED IN THE HEART

An intriguing scripture is discovered in the book of Ecclesiastes, and it clearly defines my search for God!

> *He has made everything beautiful and appropriate in its time. He has also planted eternity (a sense of divine purpose) in the human heart (a mysterious longing which nothing under the sun can satisfy, except God), ---yet man cannot find out (comprehend, grasp) what God has done (His overall plan) from the beginning to the end.* (Ecclesiastes 3:11 The Amplified Study Bible)

At age seventeen, I was on a search. My heart was restless because I wanted to experience the presence of God. This seed of eternity was planted in my heart because someone had been praying for me.

I AM PRAYING FOR YOU

As I walked into the classroom, I was delayed by a classmate who told me she had something to say. She did not wait for a response; she blurted out these words: "I have been praying for you."

"Why would you pray for me?" I asked. "I go to church every Sunday and Wednesday. I attend the morning Bible study group before classes."

Again, she said, "I have been praying for you."

Her prayers caused my heart to become more unsettled. I could not put my finger on it, but I was missing something.

GOING TO HELL

Nobody had talked to me about hell. Actually, I knew very little about it. But I sensed that I was on the path leading to this place. I wanted things to change in my life. I sought confirmation that I was headed toward heaven. So, one afternoon before basketball practice, I picked up the payphone. I called that girl, and she answered on the first ring.

"You have been praying for me. What am I missing?"

She replied that I knew about Jesus, but I did not know Him personally. I had not invited Him into my heart. Without hesitation, I said the most important prayer of my life. I prayed that I would develop a personal relationship with Jesus. I prayed for a journey with Christ that would be real. Confirmation was quick. A brilliant light shined upon me. It was so intense that I felt I could touch it. I knew I was on the right path!

I KNEW THERE WAS MORE

During the morning Bible study sessions, times of prayer were also offered. I loved hearing these students pray. They prayed with passion! They were not ashamed if their prayers were a little loud. They prayed with great expectation. They truly believed that their prayers would be answered! I could sense that these students were filled with the Holy Spirit. They were brimming with joy and life! I understood that God's Spirit was with me since I had accepted salvation. But I also knew that I could be filled with joy and full of the Holy Spirit.

So, I started my own Bible study. I looked up every scripture in the Bible concordance that referenced the Holy Spirit. One particular scripture caught my attention! The Apostle Paul visited Ephesus and spoke with some of the disciples.

"He asked them, "Did you receive the Holy Spirit when you believed (in Jesus as the Christ)?" And they said, "No, we have not even heard that there is a Holy Spirit" (Acts 19:2 The Amplified Study Bible)

They were just like me. I had never been taught about the Holy Spirit. But it would not be long before the rivers of the Holy Spirit would water the seeds of eternity in my heart!

LIVE! LAUGH! LOVE!

Jesus said that He came to give us abundant life (John 10:10).

Every time I read that scripture, I believed that abundant life could also be for me.

I asked some of those teenagers in the Bible study group to pray for me. They were glad to do so. We found a private place to pray. With great zeal, they prayed for me to be full of the joy of the Holy Spirit. They prayed for me for nearly an hour.

When they finished praying, they asked me, "Do you feel anything?"

I told them I did not feel anything. However, I have faith to believe I am full of the joy of the Holy Spirit!

FILLED WITH JOY

"And the disciples were filled with joy, and with the Holy Ghost" (Acts 13:52).

This is an amazing scripture about the disciples. They had just been expelled from the city because influential men incited some people to reject them. Yet, the disciples were not filled with anger; they were filled with the Holy Spirit. They were filled with joy. This incident reminds me of a river of joy flowing through the hearts of the disciples. The current of the river was swift enough to wash away the pain of rejection and hostility!

HOLD ON TO THE SCRIPTURES

Scriptures like this helped me stand firm in faith that I had indeed been filled with the joy of the Holy Spirit when the

20

students prayed for me. Maybe I did not feel anything, but I believed that the Holy Spirit had been poured into my heart and that joy would follow!

PRAYERS IN THE NIGHT

When I went to bed that night, I prayed a special prayer:

"Father, I am grateful that the students prayed for me. And I have prayed to be filled with the joy of the Holy Spirit! Even though I do not feel anything, by faith, I believe that I am full of the Holy Spirit."

THE NEXT MORNING

The Bible study class was in session before the start of classes. I found a spot to stand and joined in prayer. The students were praying with great passion. Suddenly, the prayer session was over, and it was time to go to class.

A couple of students came to me and asked, "Donna, have you felt the joy of the Holy Spirit since we prayed for you?"

My response was, "No." However, I assured them I believed that I had received the joy of the Holy Spirit. Then, I made my way to my locker to get ready for my first class. I had a major anatomy test in a few minutes. I had to focus on this test.

SUDDENLY

As I reached to open my locker, the presence of the Lord flowed like a river through my entire being! God's power was so strong that I actually stumbled and held onto my locker. I struggled to stand on my feet. Waves of God's presence and joy filled my heart and my mind! Never had I experienced such a river of joy like this! Peace flowed through my mind and body. People could look at me and tell that I was different. My face shined, and I bubbled over with joy. Yes, there was a river flowing through me! The force of God's presence was so powerful that I found it hard to grab my books and walk to class. When I finally got to class, it was a relief to sit down.

THE TEST

The teacher placed the test on my desk, and I looked at it. Somehow, I had to focus on the task before me. I had studied for many hours for the test, and I felt I could correctly answer the multiple-choice questions. But I had some unexpected help with the test. The light of the Holy Spirit literally highlighted each correct answer to every question. It was amazing. Even though I carefully read each question, I was drawn to the light that shone upon the correct multiple-choice questions. When the test was graded, there was a boldly marked 100 on the paper!

ENCOUNTER WITH THE HEAVENLY WATER

When the rivers of heaven flow into the hearts of men and women, it brings about real change. These waters cleanse away the pain of disappointment, condemnation, and any other negative emotions. In the story of the Samaritan woman at Jacob's well, the woman was simply going about her business when Jesus approached her (John 4:7).

"Then saith the woman of Samaria unto him, how is it that thou, being a Jew, ask drink of me, which am a woman of Samaria? For the Jews have no dealings with Samaritans" (John 4:9 KJV).

As the conversation continues, Jesus tells the woman about the water that He gives. Now, she learns about the heavenly water.

"Jesus answered and said unto her, Whosoever drinks of this water shall thirst again" (John 4:13 KJV).

"But whosoever drinks of the water that I shall give him shall never thirst; but the water that I shall give him shall be in him a well of water springing up into everlasting life" (John 4:14 KJV).

WATER FOR TIMES OF CRISIS

From this scripture, I learned to pray for rivers of living water to pour over difficult situations. At times, when I prayed for very serious situations—some required a quick change of circumstances to avert dangerous outcomes! During these times, I looked down at my abdomen, and I prayed, "Rivers of living water, spring up in me" (John 4:14) and "Heavenly Father, bring forth those springs of water within me, so I can pray effectively about this serious matter!"

WATER FOR THE WOMAN

Condemnation hung over this woman. It did not come from Jesus but from her circumstances. Jesus addressed her situation. He told her to call her husband and come (John 4:16).

Quickly, she answered, "I have no husband" (John 417).

Jesus revealed the hidden secrets of her life. He told her that she spoke correctly.

"For thou has had five husbands; and he whom thou now hast is not your husband" (John 4:18).

At that moment, the waters of heaven washed over her soul. She knew that Jesus was a holy man. She was having a divine conversation. Jesus told her that He was the Messiah, and she was grateful for this heavenly encounter!

ACTION

The joy of the Holy Spirit flooded her soul. She threw down her water bucket and ran throughout the entire village. She told the people about Jesus. Her message was delivered with passion. Many people listened and opened their hearts to Jesus because of the experience of the woman at the well. That day, revival spread to the city of Samaria, for many believed in Jesus! (John 4:40-42).

CHAPTER 2

A VIEW OF THREE SPIRITUAL RIVERS

During a time of prayer, I saw three heavenly rivers. The main river was called the "River of Living Waters." Reference to this river is found when Jesus talks with the woman at the well.

"But whosoever drinks of the water that I give him shall never thirst, but the water that I shall give him shall be in Him a well of water springing up into everlasting life" (John 4:14).

The main river flowed with clear water, and occasional waves splashed upon its shores. From the right side of the main river, another river branched off. This river was called the "River of Healing," and its waters brought healing to weary Christians. The waters refreshed the spirits, souls, and bodies of those who stepped in. The prophet Ezekiel mentions these healing waters, which flow from the temple.

"Afterward he brought me again unto the door of the house; and behold, waters issued from under the threshold of the house eastward: for the forefront of the house stood toward the east, and the waters came down from under, the right side of the house, at the south side of the altar" (Ezekiel 47:1).

Everywhere the river flowed, it brought life.

"And it shall come to pass, that everything that lives which moves, whithersoever the rivers shall come, shall live: and there shall be a very great multitude of fish, because these waters shall come thither: for they shall be healed; and everything shall live whither the river comes" (Ezekiel 47:9 KJV).

Another river branched off to the left of the main river. This river was called the "River of Revelation." Spiritual warfare requires divine revelation in order to win battles. Similarly, physical wars are won through superior intelligence. Effective strategies are revealed to us as we embrace the River of Revelation!

"The mouth of the righteous man is a well of life: but violence covers the mouth of the wicked" (Proverbs 10:11 KJV).

As I gazed upon these heavenly rivers, it became evident to me that victories in spiritual warfare can be achieved when intercessors (people of prayer) embrace them. Frequent pouring out of prayers can shift the tide of spiritual warfare!

BE REVIVED AND REFRESHED

If we expect to be effective in ministry and even in life, we must learn about restoration and allow ourselves to be restored!

Many darts of the enemy are shot with the intent of bringing discouragement. The very name of Satan reveals his true nature. "Adversary" is the meaning of the name Satan. Satan is an adversary of God. He opposes God. He is the opposite of God. The Devil is another name for the Evil One. From the Greek context, this word means "slander or false accuser."

Scripture confirmation can be found in Revelation 12:9-10:

> *And the great dragon was cast out, that old serpent, called the Devil, and Satan, which deceives the whole world: He was cast out into the earth, and his angels were cast out with him. And I heard a loud voice saying in heav-*

en, Now is come salvation, and strength, and the kingdom of God, and the power of his Christ: for the accuser of our brethren is cast down, which accused them before our God day and night.

SPIRITUAL WARFARE

Spiritual warfare is real. Even Jesus encountered the Devil in the wilderness for 40 days and 40 nights. During a time of physical weakness, the enemy launched an attack. But Jesus responded by speaking the Word of God (Matthew Chapter 4). Our real enemy is not flesh and blood, but evil spirits.

"For we wrestle not against flesh and blood., but against principalities, against powers, against the rulers of darkness of this world, against spiritual wickedness in high places" (Ephesians 6:12 KJV).

They are called fiery darts.

"Above all, taking the shield of faith, wherewith you shall be able to quench all the fiery darts of the wicked" (Ephesians 6:16).

Examples of fiery darts include the following:

- Thoughts of fear that suddenly grip a person
- Bad news coming unexpectedly
- Threats from the enemy, people, or social media
- Unjust bills
- Rejection by any means

28

QUENCH THOSE FIERY DARTS

During the times of the New Testament, fiery darts were used in warfare. The soldiers used two types of fiery arrows. One type of arrow was dipped in tar. These arrows were then set on fire and shot at the enemy. Another type of fiery arrow caused even more damage. These arrows were filled with flammable materials that were concealed from the enemy's sight. However, when the arrows hit their target, they burst into great flames. The Roman soldiers were skilled in the use of these fiery arrows. The flammable arrows were designed to resemble regular non-flammable arrows. The flammable fluids were hidden inside the arrow, so the victims could not differentiate between the two until it was too late!

FIERY DARTS OF SATAN

One of the first fiery darts used by the Devil was a question. In the Garden of Eden, the Devil approached Eve when she was away from Adam's side.

"Now the serpent was more subtile than any other beast of the field which the Lord God had made. And he said unto the woman, Yea, has God said, You shall not eat of every tree of the garden?" (Genesis 3:1 KJV).

This question caught Eve off guard, and she was tempted to eat from the wrong tree. Doubt entered her thoughts regarding the boundaries that God had set. These boundaries were created for their safety. Injecting wrong thoughts is a key strategy of the Devil. If people let down their guard, the enemy can cause fear, anxiety, anger, and confusion. The dart of "no hope" is another favorite fiery arrow of the enemy.

WAY OF ESCAPE

The shield of faith is our means of protection.

"Above all, taking the shield of faith, wherewith you shall be able to quench all the fiery darts of the wicked" (Ephesians 6:16 KJV).

When we speak God's Word, the waters of the Holy Spirit extinguish the evil arrows! A chain reaction occurs when we speak God's Word!

Speaking God's Word releases faith. The release of faith ignites the power of God. The anointing of the Holy Spirit is

31

activated, putting out the evil flames!

Consider the shields of the Roman soldiers. Frequently, the soldiers anointed their shields with oil, making them very slippery. When fiery arrows hit the slippery shields, they slid off and away from the soldier! Likewise, the anointing of the Holy Spirit diverts the fiery darts of the Devil! Those darts cannot touch us because the anointing of God creates a shield of protection.

HEDGE OF PROTECTION

Job was a man who prayed for his family. He rose early in the morning to pray for them. His prayers helped form a hedge of protection around his family, and even his possessions.

Prayers poured from this man. He also offered burnt offerings for his children. This would be like us offering prayers of repentance for ourselves and our families.

Yes, a river of intercession flowed from Job!

You may recall the story of Job. There was a day when the sons of God came to present themselves to Him. It appears that a heavenly council was in session. Then suddenly, Satan showed up among this council (Job 1:6).

A conversation is seen between God and Satan. God challenges Satan with the character of Job.

"Have you considered my servant Job? For there is none like him on earth, a blameless and upright man, one who fears God because he honors God" (Job 1:8 The Amplified Study Bible).

Satan suggests that Job has an unfair advantage because a heavenly hedge of protection surrounds him and his possessions (Job 1:10).

"Have you not put a hedge of protection around him and his house and all that he has, on every side? You have blessed the work of his hands and his possessions have increased in the land" (Job 1:10 The Amplified Study Bible).

FOR YOU

This hedge of protection is available for you, your family, and your possessions. Who will pour out rivers of intercession? Who will rise up like Job and pray? Who will take up the shield of faith and quench the fiery darts of the enemy?

CHAPTER 3

BEWARE OF RIVERS OF DESTRUCTION

Jesus offers rivers of living water for those who seek Him. The encounter of the woman at the well with Him provides confirmation (John Chapter 4).

The Devil tries to imitate Jesus. Rivers of destruction are tools of spiritual attacks released by forces of evil! The intention of these rivers is to destroy, disrupt, and delay the efforts of those who work to advance the kingdom of God.

Examples of people targeted by these evil rivers include:

- Those who preach and teach God's Word
- Worship leaders and skilled musicians
- Those who provide outreach for drug addicts, for the poor, and for the homeless
- Intercessors who pray for the church, the nation, and those in need

HOW CAN RIVERS BE DANGEROUS?

Rivers can be polluted and even poisonous. Those who drink or bathe in such rivers may become ill. One of the first examples of this in the Bible is the plague of blood. Recall that God brought plagues upon the Egyptians because they kept the children of Israel in hard bondage and slavery (Exodus Chapter 7).

> *And the Lord spoke unto Moses, Say unto Aaron, Take thy rod, and stretch out thine hand upon the waters of Egypt, upon their streams, upon their rivers, and upon their ponds, and upon all their pools of water, that they may be*

blood throughout all the land of Egypt, both in vessels of wood, and in vessels of stone. (Exodus 7:19 KJV)

For seven days, the plague of blood polluted the waters!

THE WATERS OF MARAH

It was a glorious day when Moses led the children of Israel out of Egypt. They were no longer slaves; they were a free people, and Moses was leading them to the Promised Land! However, the celebration was short-lived. Moses led the people into the wilderness of Shur (Exodus 15:22), and a source of water could not be found for three days. The people suffered as a result. Finally, they found water at Marah. Quickly, it was discovered that the water was bitter and not fit for drinking. The people became very angry at Moses and murmured against him. In desperation, Moses cried to the Lord for help.

"And he cried unto the Lord; and the Lord showed him a tree, which when he had cast into the waters were made sweet: there he made for them a statute and an ordinance, and there he proved them" (Exodus 15:25).

POISON WATERS AT JERICHO

Elisha had just witnessed his mentor Elijah being carried away to heaven in a chariot of fire with horses of fire. Now, he was the prophet to succeed Elijah (2 Kings 2:19-22). Several leaders of the city of Jericho met him as he entered the city. They told the prophet that the water of the city was bad. It was so bad that the ground remained barren and did not bring forth crops. Elisha received instructions from the Lord. He told the men to bring a new cruse and put salt in it. He took the cruse and cast the salt into the water. The Lord healed the water. Now there was no more death or barren land (2 Kings 2:21). The waters were healed!

JEALOUSY: THE RIVER OF DROWNING

It was not long after I became an ordained minister that I experienced the pain of jealousy. Like relentless waves, jealousy threatened to drown me and my first ministry of prayer if I had not responded effectively!

Not everyone was glad that I had worked for three years to become a minister. Not everyone was excited about me becoming a prayer leader. Some people spoke wrong words about me in an effort to demean me, while others tried to obstruct prayer meetings. Some even sabotaged efforts to organize corporate prayer meetings. My response was to study similar situations from the Bible. How did famous people in the Bible deal with jealousy?

The story of David taught me secrets of success that would keep those rivers of jealousy from drowning me. Even though David was kind and courteous to King Saul, he suffered from acts of jealousy. Could jealousy be an evil spirit? It is described as an evil spirit that oppressed King Saul.

King Saul was extremely jealous of David because of his popularity with the people. David returned from war, and the women of the city met him. They danced, sang songs, and played instruments of music.

"And the women answered one another as they played, and said, Saul has slain his thousands, and David his ten-thousands" (I Samuel 18:7).

King Saul was very angry about the praise the women gave to David. Scripture states that Saul eyed David from that day forward (1 Samuel 18:9). On occasions, an evil spirit would come upon Saul. Jealousy opened a door for the evil spirit. The only relief the king could find was to listen to anointed music. For this reason, David was called to play the harp in the presence of the king. When David played the harp, the evil spirit left (I Samuel 18:10). However, King Saul lost control of his emotions a few times when David played the harp. The King picked up his javelin and threw it at David with the intent to pin him to the wall. Twice, David escaped from King Saul's javelin (1 Samuel 18:11). I was impressed with David. He was a skilled man of war. He could easily have retaliated against the king, but he quietly and quickly fled from the scene.

THE SCRIPTURE THAT DEFEATS JEALOUSY

As I continued to read, I saw the scripture that gave me an advantage over jealousy. It was a scripture that would guide me many times.

"And David behaved himself wisely in all his ways; and the Lord was with him" (1 Samuel 18:14).

I made a decision to behave myself wisely when I encountered people who were filled with jealousy!

SONG OF SOLOMON & JEALOUSY

The instructions from the Song of Solomon suggest that love has the power to turn the tide of rivers of jealousy. The message I received was: "Do I love the Lord more than my desire to vindicate myself?"

"Set me as a seal upon thine heart, as a seal upon thine arm:

44

for love is strong as death; jealousy is cruel as the grave: the coals thereof are coals of fire, which has a most vehement flame" (Song of Solomon 8:6).

"Many waters cannot quench love, neither can the floods drown it; if a man would give all the substance of his house for love, it would utterly be contemned" (Song of Solomon 8:7).

Can we love God enough to trust Him to protect us from the evil river of jealousy?

WATER FROM THE MOUTH OF THE SERPENT

Persecution is a weapon of the enemy, particularly during the latter half of the tribulation. A quick review of events from Revelation Chapter 12 will confirm the vicious attacks of the enemy against God's people. This chapter will also reveal God's protection for His people! An unusual means of persecution is described in the following verse, and it includes a flood of water:

> *And when the dragon saw that he was cast unto the earth, he persecuted the woman which brought forth the man child.*
>
> *And to the woman were given two wings of a great eagle, that she might fly into the wilderness, into her place, where she is nourished for a time, and times, and half a time, from the face of the serpent.*
>
> *And the serpent cast out of his mouth water as*

*a flood after the woman, that he might cause
her to be carried away of the flood.*

*And the earth helped the woman, and the earth
opened her mouth, and swallowed up the flood
which the dragon cast out his mouth.*

*And the dragon was wroth with the woman,
and went to make war with the remnant of her
seed, which keep the commandments of God,
and have the testimony of Jesus Christ.* (Revelation 12:13-17 KJV)

The following keys will help you understand these scriptures:

- The period of time for this event is the latter time of
  the tribulation. It will be a time when evil escalates.
- The woman represents the nation of Israel.
- Her child is Christ, the Messiah.
- The flood of water is an act of persecution against the
  nation of Israel.
- The wings of the eagle suggest that God gives swift
  escape.
- The wilderness suggests a place of protection.

The main point is that the old serpent, known as Satan, uses a
river of water from his mouth to attempt to destroy the people
of Israel.

THE GOOD NEWS

Even though the persecution was intense, God intervened to protect His people. He hid them in the wilderness. Then when the flood came, He caused the earth to open up and swallow the water (Revelation 12:16).

HE LEADS US

We can trust God to lead us to the right rivers. He is the Good Shepherd. He takes care of His sheep. As we closely follow, He leads us to the still waters (Psalm 23:2).

CHAPTER 4

RIVERS THAT TURN THE HEARTS OF MEN

God can grant you favor in the most unlikely places and during the most unusual times. His favor promoted Daniel in a hostile nation, allowing him to thrive during the reigns of four kings. Favor provides us with an advantage during spiritual warfare. There were times in my life when I had to experience God's favor!

EXERCISE PHYSIOLOGY

Exercise physiology is a term that encompasses a lot of education and skill. I have always been fascinated with the study of the heart, which led me to Virginia Tech in Blacksburg, VA, where I earned my master's degree in education with an emphasis on science.

I loved everything about Virginia Tech. I was accepted into the master's program for exercise physiology, which only admitted a small group of people—about 20 in total. This diverse group came from different states and countries. There were a few times when I needed divine favor to graduate.

NEUROMUSCULAR PHYSIOLOGY

I did very well in all my classes, mostly earning As and Bs. However, in this particular class, I had a hard time scoring well on the written tests. The final exam was only a few days away, and I needed to make a grade of 100 to pass.

I prayed for God's revelation to flow. The River of Revelation is indeed available for those who seek God. Yes, I studied. As a matter of fact, I studied all night for the exam. But I also prayed for the Holy Spirit to help me answer the questions correctly. When I took the exam, answers to the questions came to me with ease! The final exam grade was proof of God's River of Revelation. One hundred was the score on my exam, surely surprising even the professor!

APPROVAL OF MY THESIS

The research thesis was completed, addressing the hypothesis with real numbers from several rounds of testing. I was ready to graduate—all I needed was the final approval of the main professor. His signature was all that was required. However, he just did not seem to have thirty minutes to give to me. During these thirty minutes, he would sign the thesis and confirm my graduation.

It was December, only about 10 days before the college closed for the winter session. If he did not sign, I would have to pay for another term of tuition and return to college. Additionally, I would miss a major job opportunity that I had pursued.

WARFARE

For me, this was a time of spiritual warfare, and it wasn't really fair. I had devoted over 2 years of my life, as well as finances, to graduate. A river of prayer was needed to turn this tide. As I prayed earnestly about this matter, the Holy Spirit gave me a strategy. I received my answer from the Parable of the Woman and the Unjust Judge. Jesus taught this parable. It teaches about the power of praying with perseverance, which gave victory to this poor widow.

She had a legal case that required the intervention of a judge. Day after day, she came to him. He kept ignoring her and putting her off (Luke 18:1-8), but she kept coming. Finally, he realized that the only way to get rid of her was to address the case.

"Yet, because this widow troubles me, I will avenge her, lest by her continual coming she weary me" (Luke 18:5).

LIKE THIS WOMAN

Like this woman, I came to the professor's door every day. I would sit outside his office door at 7:30 a.m. During the first week, he would walk past me and let other students into his office. However, there came a day when he could no longer ignore me. He finally welcomed me into his office, and that's when he sealed my graduation.

THE DREAM

King Nebuchadnezzar had a dream that put his astrologers, magicians, and sorcerers to the test.

"And the King said unto them, I have dreamed a dream, and my spirit was troubled to know the dream" (Daniel 2:3).

The king's advisors were skilled in the art of interpreting dreams. Eagerly, they asked him to repeat the dream. However, they encountered an unexpected problem. The king could not remember the dream. Yet, he expected them to tell him both the dream and the interpretation.

If they failed, they would face death!

"The King answered and said to the Chaldeans, The thing is gone from me: if you will not make known unto me the dream,

with the interpretation thereof, you will be cut in pieces, and your houses shall be made a dunghill" (Daniel 2:5 KJV).

On the other hand, if the advisors were successful, they would be greatly rewarded (Daniel 2:6). In their state of fear, the Chaldeans told the king that there was not a man on Earth who could tell him his dream (Daniel 2:10).

ANGRY

The king grew furious with his advisors and threatened to destroy all the wise men of Babylon (Daniel 2:12). Knowing that Daniel and his friends were different because they worshipped only one God, the advisors turned to him for help.

DANIEL BEFORE THE KING

Daniel made a formal request to speak to the king. He told the king to give him time, and he would be able to tell the dream and its interpretation. Prayer was Daniel's first action! He told his three friends about the matter and requested prayer. Rivers of prayer flowed from the hearts and mouths of these men. They prayed fervently about this matter (Daniel 2:17 KJV).

IN THE NIGHT

During the prayer watches of the night, God's presence is so powerful. The study of the Scriptures shows that great acts of deliverance occur during night watches! I recall the times when I prayed in all-night prayer meetings at the Voice of Praise Church. There were great releases of the Holy Spirit. Often, during night prayers, I encountered the supernatural presence of God. I could feel His Spirit, and angels were very active during these prayer meetings!

Daniel received God's intervention during the night.

"Then was the secret revealed unto Daniel in a night vision, Then Daniel blessed the God of heaven" (Daniel 2: 19 KJV).

A HAPPY ENDING

When Daniel stood before the king, he told both the dream and the interpretation. Daniel gave God the credit for his skill.

"He reveals the deep and secret things: he knows what is in the darkness, and the light dwells with him" (Daniel 2:22).

The king was very pleased with Daniel, and his advisors were happy. Daniel and his friends were also filled with joy.

WHAT ABOUT YOU?

- Are you facing a difficult situation?
- Do things seem impossible to you?
- Do you feel as if you have come up against a wall?
- Are you praying for someone who has strayed from God?
- Do you need God to turn the hearts of people to favor you?

CHAPTER 5

THE FIGHT FOR FINANCES

It should be no surprise that the enemy delights in disrupting a person's financial flow. After all, Jesus refers to Him as a thief.

"The thief comes not but for to steal, and to kill, and to destroy: I am come that they may have life, and that they might have it more abundantly" (John 10:10).

Have you found yourself in a fight for financial stability? Did unexpected bills arrive? Did the car suddenly need repairs? Did an accident or illness occur?

This fight for finances began as early as the Garden of Eden. Not only did Adam and Eve enjoy an abundance of food, but dominion was also given to them in the Garden!

> *And God created man in his own image, in the image of God created he him; male and female created he them. And God blessed them, and God said unto them, Be fruitful, and multiply, and replenish the earth, and subdue it: and have dominion over the fish of the sea, and over the fowl of the air, and over every living thing that moves upon the earth.* (Genesis 1:27-28 KJV)

THE EYE OF THE ENEMY

Apparently, the enemy watched Adam and Eve from a distance. He saw their prosperity and the authority granted to them. As he watched, he devised a plan to steal the blessings that God had given Adam and Eve! The enemy also watches you. He looks for ways to cause you financial distress!

One day, the enemy saw his chance. The woman was separated from the man, and he could talk to her alone! The rest of the story is well-known. Satan convinced the woman to eat the forbidden fruit. In an act of disobedience to God, she ate the fruit. She also convinced Adam to eat the fruit (Genesis 3:1–13). Immediately, the consequences of disobedience were felt. Their eyes were opened, and they sewed fig leaves together to make clothes (Genesis 1:7). Then, for the first time, they were afraid of God. When they heard God walking in the garden, they hid (Genesis 3:8). Even today, people try to hide from God when they sin. Instead of turning to Him in prayer and repentance, they run from Him. What a dangerous situation they place themselves in when they hide from God. They remove themselves from God's protective hedge and are vulnerable to the attacks of the enemy.

THE TASTE OF LACK

Adam and Eve were cast out of the garden. There was no chance to return, for an angelic being protected the garden.

"So he drove out the man; and he placed at the east of the garden of Eden, Cherubim and a flaming sword which turned every way, to keep the way of the tree of life" (Genesis 3:24).

Outside of the Garden of Eden, life was harder. When they attempted to farm the land, thistles and thorns grew. The labor was so hard that sweat flowed. Poverty, lack, and struggle were now real enemies.

"Thorns also and thistles shall it bring forth to thee: and thou shalt eat the herb of the field. In the sweat of thy face shalt

thou eat bread, till thou return unto the ground; for out of it was thou taken: for dust thou art, and unto dust shalt thou return" (Genesis 3:18-19 KJV).

JESUS CHANGED THINGS

Jesus gave both authority and strategies to win the battles of financial struggle! He preached a new message and ignited hope in the hearts of the oppressed. My financial victories began to come when I embraced the following scripture:

"The thief comes not but for to steal, and to kill, and to destroy: I am come that they might have life, and that they might have it more abundantly" (John 10:10).

Yes, there is a river of plenty that flows for us to enjoy.

"There is a river, the streams whereof shall make glad the city of God, the holy place of the tabernacles of the Most High" (Psalm 46:4).

HEAVEN'S ECONOMY

There is no recession in heaven. There is no lack in heaven. Testimonies of those who have died and were resuscitated confirm the riches of heaven. One man's testimony inspired me as a young Christian. He was the guest speaker at our weekly Bible study. He had worked as a truck driver. After his heavenly encounter, he also did inspirational speaking for conferences, churches, and Bible studies. He died on the operating table during a period of cardiac arrest for about 5 to 6 minutes.

When he talked about heaven, he mentioned a beautiful pathway with glorious flowers on each side. The flowers were brilliant in color and released aromatic fragrances, vibrant in red, blue, and yellow. He remembered the strong, sweet smells of those flowers.

He saw green rolling hills all around him, and in the distance, he saw a city of gold. The light of the city was so bright that it shined everywhere; there was no darkness.

A defibrillator was used to shock his heart. After a few shocks, he recovered. Now, he was back in the hospital room, and the doctors and nurses saw the light on his face. They listened as he told them about his trip to heaven.

STREETS OF GOLD

The Lord's Prayer assures us that we can pray for God's will to be done on the earth, as it is in heaven (Matthew 6:10). And we know that Jesus came to give us life and more abundant life (John 10:10). Also, from the Lord's Prayer, we can ask Him to give us our daily bread. He expects us to pray for the things that we need.

A glimpse of heaven reveals some of the great treasures found there! The apostle John is given a view of New Jerusalem. He sees this glorious city descending out of heaven from God (Revelation 21:10). He speaks of the streets of gold.

"And the twelve gates, were twelve pearls; every several gate was of one pearl: and the street of the city was pure gold, as it were transparent glass" (Revelation 21:21 KJV).

PRAY FOR THE RIVER

We can pray for the river of blessings to flow upon us. Such a prayer may be as simple as the following:

"Father, in Jesus' name, I remind You of Your Word. Jesus has come to give me abundant life. In faith, I ask for this abundant life. Release rivers of blessings for me and my family. Also, I ask for provision for our daily needs."

OPEN THE GATES OF BRASS AND BARS OF IRON

Dams are constructed to prohibit the flow of water. Likewise, in the spiritual realm, the enemy attempts to hinder the flow of financial blessings. Many ministers can tell you about the spiritual strategies of the enemy to withhold financial blessings. This is a prayer that I prayed for my husband.

When we were just married, he applied for a job that he truly wanted. Indeed, he was highly qualified. However, day after day went by and we heard nothing from the company. I began to pray for God to open the gates of brass and the bars of iron that were withholding this opportunity (Psalm 107:16). I reminded the Father that His Word does not return to Him void.

> *For as the rain comes down, and the snow from heaven, and returns not thither, but waters the earth and makes it bring forth and bud, that it may give seed to the sower, and bread to the eater. So shall my word be that goes forth out of my mouth, it shall not return unto me void, but it shall accomplish that which I please, and it shall prosper in the*

thing whereto I sent it. (Isaiah 55:10-11)

Like a river, I was pouring forth God's Word in prayer. Daily, I was releasing a flow of prayer. Within a very short period of time, my husband received a call from the company. He got the job. This job was a divine opportunity for us. Through this job, we met wonderful friends who continue to support us!

PAY YOUR TAXES

There is a story that I recall about taxes being due. Jesus and Peter traveled to the town of Capernaum. While they were there, some tax collectors approached them. These men asked Peter if Jesus paid taxes (Matthew 17:24). "Yes," was the answer. Peter then went to Jesus and informed him about the tax collectors.

Jesus told Peter that they would indeed pay their taxes. They would pay the taxes to avoid causing offense. Jesus provided Peter with instructions to obtain the money needed to pay the taxes.

"Go to the sea, and cast a hook. Open the mouth of the very first fish and you will find a piece of money" (Matthew 17:27).

Peter took that money and paid their taxes!

KEEP THE RIVER FLOWING

God has given us His ways for keeping the river of financial blessings flowing! His ways are tried and proven. His ways lead to success and victory. His ways lead us to abundant life. Remember that Jesus told us He came so that we could have abundant life (John 10:10).

PLANT A SEED

The principle of sowing and reaping was familiar to me. In my first book, I talk about being raised on a farm. Every spring, we planted strawberries, beans, squash, sugar cane, and other vegetables carefully in the fertile ground. During the fall, we sold the harvest at markets. I understood that if we did not take the time and effort to plant, there would be no plants growing from the ground! Likewise, in the spiritual realm, our seeds of giving, caring, praying, and encouraging produce much fruit. When we plant these spiritual seeds on a consistent basis, we will reap time after time. Unexpected financial blessings and opportunities will come our way.

"Give, and it shall be given unto you; good measure, pressed down, and shaken together, and running over, shall men give into your bosom. For with the same measure that you mete withal it shall be measured to you again" (Luke 6:38 KJV).

I especially like to give to those who have suffered from natural disasters. The American Red Cross is a favorite organization for me. I can be assured that my donation will help those in great need.

"He that has pity upon the poor lends unto the Lord; and that which he has given will he pay him again" (Proverbs 19:17).

My mom has provided a role model for helping the poor. I have seen her help poor children by providing lunch money for them at school. During the holidays, she buys gifts and food for the needy in the community! In addition to giving donations on a consistent basis, I also tithe from my paychecks. I realize that people have different opinions about tithing. I do respect their beliefs. When I was a child, I saw my dad tithe. His faithfulness in this area inspired me. In addition, my husband strongly believes in tithing. Giving 10 percent to God, only seems right. Our tithes and offerings have an impact on the spiritual realm. Financial doors of opportunity and favor are opened for us and our children!

> *Bring ye all the tithes into the storehouse, that there may be meat in mine house, and prove me now herewith, saith the Lord of hosts, if I will not open you the windows of heaven, and pour you out a blessing, that there shall not room enough to receive it. And I will rebuke the devourer for your sakes, and he shall not destroy the fruits of your ground; neither shall your vine cast her fruit before the time in the field, said the Lord of hosts.* (Malachi 3:10-11 KJV)

JESUS WATCHES THE OFFERING PLATE

The story of the widow with two mites fascinates me. It starts by describing Jesus as standing by the treasury. This could be considered the offering plate. He watched people come and give their offerings. I believe that even today, He watches us as we give and looks at the intents of our hearts!

Several rich men came and threw in large amounts of money. Attitudes of pride were the basis of their giving. They gave in such a manner that people could see what they had given (Mark 12:41-44).

Then suddenly, a poor widow went quietly to the offering plate. She tried not to draw any attention to herself. When she got to the offering plate, she saw Jesus. Quickly, she threw in two mites. The mite was worth about one-eighth of a cent.

Jesus noted her offering and the pure intent of her heart. To this day, she is famous and provides great inspiration.

Even a small amount of money is valuable in the eyes of Jesus when given with a true heart!

> *And he called unto him his disciples, and saith unto them, Verily I say unto you, that this poor widow has cast more in, than all they which have cast into the treasury. For all they did cast in of their abundance; but she of her want did cast in all that she had, even all her living.* (Mark 12:43-44 KJV)

MONEY COME

As a young Christian, I had never considered that I could pray for money to come to me. This all changed when I met an older lady named Irene. She was a participant in the exercise class I taught for seniors. Even though she was in her 80s, she was full of life. She had a strong Christian faith and was quick to pray for those who asked for her prayers. One day, she came to pray for me. She prayed that money would come! She did not know I was facing a financial need. She was prompted by the Holy Spirit to pray this prayer. Yes, my financial need was resolved as money came!

Today, I frequently pray over our bills and other needs. I stretch my hands over the bills and pray for money to come. I do not just pray; I work hard and invest wisely. And often, I see the Father provide for our financial needs! Refunds may come, or my husband will be given additional work hours, or gifts will appear in the mail! Yes, rivers of blessings flow for those who ask!

CHAPTER 6

THE SPIRITUAL WEAPON OF JOY

There is a powerful spiritual weapon that puts the Devil on the run. However, this weapon is often overlooked. Many desperately need this weapon: joy. If you lack joy, ask for it! We are called to come to the Father in prayer and make specific requests. Be clear and specific about your needs.

"And in that day you shall ask me nothing, Verily, verily, I say unto you, Whatsoever you shall ask the Father in my name, he will give it to you. Hitherto have you asked nothing in my name; ask, and you shall receive, that your joy may be full" (John 16:23-24 KJV).

When we are full of joy, we are filled with strength to overcome the enemy.

OLD FAITHFUL FAMOUS GEYSER

On a vacation to Yellowstone, I was privileged to witness the power emitted by Old Faithful. Explosive bursts of water shot straight up from the ground. A tourist guide will tell you that Old Faithful erupts about 20 times a day. Most eruptions last from 1.5 to 5 minutes. The height of these eruptions ranges from 130 to 140 feet on average. Steam from the geyser is very hot, about 130 to 140 degrees Fahrenheit. Like a geyser, when joy is released, bursts of power spring forth. The power of joy delivers direct hits upon the demonic forces!

JOY FOR NEHEMIAH

Nehemiah was the governor of Jerusalem. He served as a personal cupbearer to the Persian King, Artaxerxes I. The setting of this famous story occurred between the years 464 B.C. to 423 B.C. Nehemiah was appointed governor of the province and given the authority to rebuild the walls of the City of Jerusalem. Nehemiah and his labor force were harassed by three enemies who made many attempts to obstruct the rebuilding of the walls.

Possessed with spiritual strength, Nehemiah led his team to rebuild the walls in a remarkably short period of time. In just 52 days, the Jews rebuilt the walls of Jerusalem! During the work of rebuilding the walls, they had to protect themselves from any sudden attacks, working with a weapon in one hand!

"They which built on the wall, and they that bare burdens, with those that laded, every one with one of his hands wrought in the work, and with the other hand held a weapon" (Nehemiah 4:17 KJV).

From Nehemiah, we learn that the "joy of the lord is your strength!" (Nehemiah 8:10). The Devil is intimidated by those who are filled with joy!

MISERABLE

There was a time in my life that I was miserable. It was also during this time that I suffered from insomnia. It was my first year in college. In addition to studying for some difficult classes, I also played sports. I did not have a spare moment.

One of my classes required a lot of time to complete the assignments. I remember sitting in my room and praying this prayer:

"Father, You know that I love You, and have followed You for several years. And those were good years. But now in my present situation, I am very unhappy. I want to love, to laugh, and to live again. I want to have abundant life as Jesus promised."

I went to the church to pray. The pastor met me there and listened as I poured out my distress. I wanted someone to pray for me. Also, I wanted to be healed of insomnia.

TO THE RIVER

At the Holston River, I was healed of all emotional distress and insomnia. At a beautiful prayer room by the river, people prayed for me. I remember seeing a brilliant light shining upon me. I also saw Jesus standing over me! When I left the place of prayer by the river, I felt joy flood into my heart. It had been a long time since I enjoyed this feeling. That night, when I went to bed, I fell asleep as soon as my head hit the pillow!

THE LORD LAUGHS

"The wicked plots against the just, and gnashes upon him with his teeth" (Psalm 37:12 KJV).

"The Lord shall laugh at him: for he sees that his day is coming" (Psalm 37:13 KJV).

The Devil does not like anyone to laugh at him. Laughter intimidates him. Have you watched professional wrestling? If so, you have heard how each wrestler taunts the other. A person filled with joy and laughter, even during difficult times, is a challenge for the Devil! Like a mighty gushing river, joy bubbles over.

JOY WINS THE BATTLE FOR JEHOSHAPHAT

A messenger came to the king and warned him that a great multitude was coming against the nation of Judah. This multitude consisted of several armies.

"It came to pass after this also, that the children of Moab, and the children of Ammon, and with them other beside of the Ammonites, came against Jehoshaphat to battle" (2 Chronicles 1:1 KJV).

King Jehoshaphat was a righteous king. He prayed to the Lord and commanded the nation to fast. His prayer was powerful. From his prayer, we learn a very important key to utilize in spiritual warfare!

"O our God, wilt thou not judge them? For we have no might against this great company that comes against us; neither know we what to do: but our eyes are upon you" (2 Chronicles 20:12).

WHEN YOU DO NOT KNOW WHAT TO DO

When you face great challenges, you may wonder what to do. Sometimes answers do not seem to come quickly enough. The same strategy that worked for King Jehoshaphat will work for you: put your eyes on God! Get your eyes off the problem and look to God. He has the answers. How do you do this? You come to God in prayer, just like the king. Pray like the king.

"Father, I am facing a great challenge. And I do not know what to do. However, I put my eyes on You!"

RELEASING THE WEAPON OF JOY

Armies of the flesh were coming after the king and the nation of Judah. Additionally, spiritual armies of demonic forces were working behind the scenes. Releasing the weapon of joy would defeat both armies.

In answer to King Jehoshaphat's prayer, the Lord gave a battle strategy. The singers were to go before the army of Judah. In addition, the Lord gave them great assurance.

"You shall not need to fight in this battle: set yourselves, stand still, and see the salvation of the Lord: set yourselves, stand you still, and see the salvation of the Lord with you, O Judah and Jerusalem: fear not, nor be dismayed; tomorrow go out against them: for the Lord will be with you" (2 Chronicles 20:17 KJV).

JOY! JOY! JOY!

The army danced and sang with joy. This joy was released into the atmosphere. The Lord set ambushments against the children of Ammon, Moab, and Mount Seir (2 Chronicles 20:22 KJV). An ambushment is a metaphor for angels! The enemies became confused and began to fight against each other. They killed each other.

When the children of Israel came to the battle site, they saw the dead bodies of their enemies. Also, they found precious jewels and other riches, and they gathered these spoils. Joy was released into the atmosphere.

When the singers praised the Lord, both physical and spiritual ears heard them. The armies that came against Judah, heard the joyful sounds. They became confused and destroyed each other! Demonic spirits heard the joyful sounds, and they were paralyzed! We can also change spiritual atmospheres with joy!

THE GOODNESS OF THE LORD

When people see the Lord releasing goodness toward them, they are more receptive to Him! When they witness their sick child being brought back to health, they are more inclined to seek the Lord. When a financial crisis is averted by a miracle of God, they are touched by His goodness. When a job opportunity is offered to them, they experience joy and give thanks to God!

"Or despisest thou the riches of his goodness and forbearance and long-suffering; not knowing that the goodness of God leads you to repentance?" (Romans 2:4 KJV).

TIMES OF JOY IN MY LIFE

There are many incidents that brought me great joy:

- Graduation from high school and college
- Vacation trips

- My wedding day
- The birth of a child

But I recall great joy during church events when people responded to the altar call. Seeing loved ones, friends, and others turn their lives to God caused me to be filled with immense joy. Tears of happiness flooded down my cheeks! Angels also express great joy when people turn to God.

"Likewise, I say unto you, there is joy in the presence of the angels of God over one sinner that repents" (Luke 15:10 KJV).

CHAPTER 7

REVERSING HOSTILE SPIRITUAL ATMOSPHERES

Often, Jesus changed people's lives. He raised the dead, healed the blind, delivered people from demonic oppression, fed over 5000 people with two fish and five loaves of bread, and calmed a raging sea that frightened His disciples.

ATMOSPHERES

Atmospheres can be shaped by weather. Also, they can be defined as the tone or mood of a place. For example, in a room with a business meeting, the atmosphere may be tense. On the other hand, in a room with a wedding, the atmosphere may be joyful. However, pleasant atmospheres can suddenly change when a negative or hostile person enters the room. Without warning, a happy atmosphere can turn into fear if bad news is reported.

MT. ROGERS: THE HIGHEST POINT IN VIRGINIA

In my younger days, I loved hiking to the top of Mt. Rogers. It was about 9.5 miles round trip. It was a delight to tell my friends that I had hiked to the highest mountain in Virginia! The views from the mountain are spectacular! Additionally, there are wild ponies that allow tourists to pet them on the head.

About half a mile to the top of the mountain, the air becomes thinner. The amount of oxygen for breathing is less. The breathing rate significantly increases. Also, at higher altitudes, the tops of the trees are bare of leaves. Most of the time, when we reached the top of the mountain, we ate our packed lunches. We also took pictures of the marker for the highest point in Virginia. Then we headed back down the mountain.

Several times, my dad told me to never get caught on the top of the mountain in a thunderstorm. He described the violent nature of these high-altitude storms. He also mentioned that these storms burst forth suddenly, often without warning!

I remember taking a few friends from Bluefield to the mountain. They were so excited. They wanted to take pictures. And they wanted to tell their friends that they hiked to the highest point in Virginia. One of the friends had a little dog. I wondered how that tiny dog could possibly make it up the steep mountain. Often when I looked behind me, I saw the owner carrying the little dog!

Finally, we got to a hiker's station. It was a small building with a large porch. Hikers could go inside and find refuge from the rain. We were about one-fourth of a mile to the top. I looked to the skies. Suddenly, I saw dark clouds begin to form. I told the group that we had to go back quickly. However, they begged me to take them to the top. They wanted to tell their family and friends that they made it to the top.

We reached the top of the mountain. Quickly, we took pictures of the marker. And we started back down the mountain. In just a few minutes, a violent storm burst upon us. We had just passed the hikers' station and had no way to shelter from the storm!

Lightning struck all around us. Trees were hit by the lightning and fell across our path! Water poured from the skies. The water quickly covered our ankles. The little dog hugged close to its owner.

The visitors cried out, "What can we do?"

I replied, "The only thing we can do is get off this mountain."

Finally, we reached a small cave and stayed under it. From the cave, we could look down the mountain. No storm was there. This was a lesson for me. I learned that hostile atmospheres could burst forth without warning! And later in my life, I would learn that this is also true in the spiritual realm!

WHY REVERSE SPIRITUAL ATMOSPHERES

Hostile spiritual atmospheres oppress people and hold them in spiritual chains of bondage. In addition, such atmospheres can escalate to levels of violence. Jesus reversed hostile spiritual atmospheres and set people free.

MY NAME IS LEGION

This story from the New Testament provides ample proof of how hostile spiritual atmospheres oppress people and even territories! One day, when Jesus and His disciples stepped off their boat, they were met by a wild-looking man. Just imagine the scene: his hair stood up on his head; his eyes flashed with anger, and his face was filled with rage. He ran from the tombs, screaming and ranting, not wearing any clothes, and rushed toward Jesus and the disciples (Luke 8:28).

I'm sure the disciples wondered why Jesus came to this region known as the country of the Gadarenes. There were no crowds to welcome Him, no friendly faces. It seemed that Jesus came to rescue this one man. Likewise, Jesus will come to rescue you. He knows how to find you and understands the troubles you face.

THE ENCOUNTER

I remember when my family and I went on a cruise ship. We visited a famous southern island just below the United States. We were curious about getting off the boat. Questions flooded our minds: What kind of people would we meet? What would the scenery reveal?

If we had seen this man running from the tombs toward us, we might have rushed back onto the cruise ship! When this tormented man came close to Jesus, he appeared to be in his right mind for a few minutes. He ran to Jesus and worshipped Him. But quickly, the demons took over, screaming through the man's voice.

"What have I to do with you, Jesus, thou Son of the most high. I beseech you, torment me not" (Luke 8:28).

Can you see horror on the face of the demon as Jesus addressed him? The very presence of Jesus torments the Devil. Jesus asked, "What is your name?"

"Legion" replied the demon. "For we are many" (Luke 8:30).

A legion was known to be a Roman army unit consisting of as many as six thousand soldiers! The demons begged Jesus not to send them out into the deep (Luke 8:31). This translation of the word refers to the underworld. This was known as the abode of the dead (Romans 10:7).

TERRITORIAL DEMONIC SPIRITS

The demons begged Jesus to let them enter a herd of swine. When they entered the herd of about 2000, they ran violently down a cliff into the sea (Mark 5:13). More than likely, a territorial demonic spirit or spirits ruled this region in the spiritual realm. Evidence for this is seen when the demons entered the herd of swine. This man needed to be set free. The demons inside him posed a great threat to him and the community. Jesus heard the cry of his heart. With compassion, Jesus commanded the demons to leave the man. Now he was

86

free and in his right mind! (Mark 5:15 KJV).

"And they come to Jesus, and see him that was possessed with the devil, and had the legion, sitting, and clothed, and in his right mind: and they were afraid" (Mark 5:15 KJV).

DO YOU FACE HOSTILE SPIRITUAL ATMOSPHERES?

If you are facing difficult situations, come to the One who can calm the storms. Like the oppressed man, run to Jesus and ask Him to intervene!

"Wherefore he is able also to save them to the uttermost that come unto God by him, seeing he ever lives to make intercession for them" (Hebrews 7:25).

PERMEATING THE ATMOSPHERE

When Jesus entered the room, both demons and people took notice. The power of the Holy Spirit flowed through Him like a mighty river. Likewise, we also emit a distinct impression wherever we go. If we have the river of the Holy Spirit flowing through us, there will be a release of His power and nature. The fruits of the Spirit will be manifested. These include love, joy, peace, and faith (Galatians 5:22-23). We are described as a fragrance in the book of 2 Corinthians.

For we are the sweet fragrance of Christ (which ascends) to God, (discerning both) among those who are being saved and among those who are perishing. To the latter one an aroma from death to death (a fatal, offensive odor), but to the other an aroma from life to life (a vital fragrance, living and fresh). And who is adequate and sufficiently qualified for these things. (2 Corinthians 2:15-16 The Amplified Study Bible)

Those who love God and serve Him are refreshed by our presence. However, those who oppose God and serve their own interests release an unpleasant feeling in the atmosphere. Also, demonic spirits are uncomfortable around us.

I have experienced this often. There are times when I have entered meetings. No sooner had I sat down, than frowns appeared on the faces of attendees who serve their own desires. On the other hand, there are times when I have walked into prayer meetings and felt engulfed in peace. I felt accepted and vital to the group.

HEALING AROMAS

It is a proven fact that when certain aromas are released, healing benefits occur! Some amazing benefits of sweet fragrances include:

- Sweet perfumes enhance one's mood and keep stress away. Some of the scents that calm the mind are citrus, floral, and winter spice perfumes.
- Insomnia can be relieved with certain scents. Lavender and jasmine are scents that help soothe and induce sleep.
- Focus can also be improved with certain scents. Examples include peppermint, spearmint, lemon, and rosemary.

- Headaches are relieved by some perfumes. Lavender, chamomile, and eucalyptus are proven aids.
- Boosting energy levels is a benefit of other perfumes. Peppermint, sweet orange, lemon, and spearmint are helpful for energy boosts.

When engaging in serious writing, I often light aromatic candles. The scent of these candles helps me relax and reminds me of the beautiful aromas in heaven.

THE AROMA BEFORE A BATTLE

I am convinced that when we engage in intercessory battles over the souls of people, and even the destiny of nations, we emit a formidable presence to the demonic spiritual realm (2 Corinthians 2:15-16). When we pray the Scriptures with faith and power, a powerful essence is released toward the enemy. Consider the fresh scent just before a physical storm. Many times, I have noticed this fresh scent just before a storm erupts, especially when lightning is present. Since science is one of my favorite subjects, I sought answers about this fresh smell. A curious person can simply search the internet for information about storms. The ozone layer is the source of the fresh and sweet scent before a storm. When lightning strikes, it splits the nitrogen and oxygen molecules in the atmosphere, resulting in nitric oxide, which then forms ozone. The wind carries this scent just before the rain begins. Wow! Does this sound like spiritual warfare?

Remember King Jehoshaphat's army? When the people began to sing and praise, the Lord created unexpected attacks upon the invading armies. The enemies became confused and disoriented, and they destroyed each other! When we pray God's scriptures, we release a great source of power!

"For the Word of God is quick, and powerful, and sharper than any two-edged sword, piercing even to the dividing asunder of soul and spirit, and of the joints and marrow, and is a discerner of the thoughts and intents of the heart" (Hebrews 4:12 KJV).

CHAPTER 8

RIVERS IN THE NIGHT

I am convinced that there are some victories we may never experience if we do not pray in the night watches. There was a time in my life when great challenges confronted me, and it was critical that I responded to various situations carefully. I prayed every type of prayer that I knew. But victories did not come; help did not come; in fact, things seemed to get worse. "Ask for wisdom," was a scripture that I discovered (James 1:5), and that is exactly what I did! I received a successful strategy: to pray in the night watches, specifically the fourth watch of the night. The fourth watch of the night starts at 3:00 a.m. and lasts for three hours, ending at 6:00 a.m. I was to pray this night watch for a few weeks, so I adjusted my schedule to go to bed earlier, determined to obey the Lord in this matter.

The first night was exciting and not difficult to pray. I walked as I prayed for most of the watch to stay awake. I opened my Bible and prayed scripture verses. This three-hour night watch went by fast, and I found that I needed more time to pray over all concerns. I was not disappointed. On the very first day of the night watch, amazing victories occurred. Things began to change, and the tide turned in my favor. I had learned to pray with rivers of intercession in the night watches!

ADVANTAGES OF PRAYING IN THE NIGHT

One major advantage of praying in the night watches is that it puts you one step ahead of the Devil. Often, in times of prayer, I felt as if I was on the defensive. When you pray in the night watch, you launch an offensive attack. You score victories. You set up a hedge of protection for yourself and your family. I like being on the offensive end. Other intercessors who regularly pray in the night watches have reported the following benefits:

- God's presence flows like a river during the night.
- The presence of the Holy Spirit is very intense.
- There are less distractions at night.
- The faith of the intercessor is strengthened.
- Many state they feel great peace in the night.
- Others tell of physical healings during night prayers.
- Wisdom and instructions from the Holy Spirit are often received.

"I will bless the Lord, who has given me counsel: my reins also instruct me in the night seasons" (Psalm 16:7 KJV).

DOUBLE POWER

"Yet the Lord will command his loving-kindness in the daytime, and in the night his song shall be with me, and my prayer unto the God of my life" (Psalm 42:8).

From this scripture, I see two major actions occurring. First, I am pouring out my heart to the Lord, praying His promises from the Scriptures. There is a release of faith-based prayers.

The second action is Him singing His song over me! I believe that these are songs of deliverance. Heaven is involved in this time of prayer, and King David speaks of these songs of deliverance.

"Thou are my hiding place; thou shalt preserve me from trouble; thou shalt compass me about with songs of deliverance. Selah" (Psalm 32:7).

A hedge of protection surrounds my household, and angels defend our interests. They are released to bring answers to prayers. When we speak God's Word over situations, angels are activated.

"Bless the Lord, you his angels, that excel in strength, that do his commandments, hearkening unto the voice of his word" (Psalm 103:20 KJV).

NO NIGHT PRAYER = FEW VICTORIES

Once again, I emphasize my conviction that we may never experience certain victories if we do not pray in the night watches! There are several examples of individuals who achieved great victories when they engaged in the night watches. Jesus prayed all night on several occasions.

"And it came to pass in those days, that he went out into the mountain to pray, and continued all night in prayer to God" (Luke 6:12 KJV).

A couple of significant things happened after Jesus prayed all night. The first major action was choosing His twelve disciples. These were men who would follow Him from town to town, assist in teaching multitudes, and carry His message after His death. Indeed, this was a crucial decision, one that would not be made without a night of prayer.

Next, a group of people came to hear Him. He healed those vexed with unclean spirits, and virtue flowed out of Him, healing them all (Luke 6:19). This virtue was a supernatural power that flowed from Jesus. It was so great that it healed everyone who came to Him.

When we pray in the night watches, we too will be granted wisdom to make important decisions. Our faith will be strengthened, and our prayers will be filled with power.

JACOB WRESTLED ALL NIGHT

"And Jacob was left alone, and there wrestled a man with him until the breaking of the day" (Genesis 32:24 KJV).

Imagine an angel coming to Jacob at night, and suddenly, he and the angel wrestle all night. The angel was urgent to leave before dawn, as spirits hasten to arrive at their abode before the break of day. Some confirmation is provided by the following verse.

"And he (angel) said, Let me go, for the day breaks. And he (Jacob) said, I will not let you go, except thou bless me" (Genesis 32:26).

A couple of lessons are revealed from this prayer event. Like Jacob, we should be willing to wrestle in prayer during the night. Also, we should ask for a blessing to be released to us. In this instance, Jacob's name was changed. No longer was he a deceiver; now, he was known as Israel. This was a majestic name, signifying that he was a prince who had power with God and men (Genesis 32:28). When you become a regular intercessor in the night hours, both heaven and hell will know your name.

PRAYER WATCHES IN THE NIGHT

Prayers in the night release a mighty river of the Holy Spirit. Intercessors cry out to God with great passion. I remember times when we camped by a river at night. We loved hearing the sound of the river throughout the night. The prayers of the intercessors throughout the night also release a sound of victory!

"Arise, cry aloud in the night. At the beginning of the night watches. Pour out your heart like water. Before the presence of the Lord; Lift up your hands to Him. For the life of your little ones who faint from hunger at the end of every street" (Lamentations 2:19 The Amplified Study Bible).

A HEAVENLY VIEW

As I prepared for this chapter of the book, I saw a beautiful scene during a time of prayer. I witnessed a full moon hovering over a river, with small clouds of fog hanging above it. In the midst of the fog, there was a bright light. As my eyes focused on the light, a sense of peace flooded my soul. Moreover, I saw angels traveling up the stream. Life was flowing from that river, and revelation knowledge was released from the bright light. The angels were receiving prayer assignments and would soon depart for their missions.

THE FOUR WATCHES OF THE NIGHT

The following scriptures provide a brief summary of the four watches of the night.

"Watch you therefore: for you know not when the master of the house comes, at even (First Watch, 6:00 p.m. to 9:00 p.m.), or at midnight (Second Watch, 9:00 p.m. to 12:00 a.m.), or at the cockcrowing, (12:00 a.m. to 3:00 a.m.), (Third Watch), or in the early morning (Fourth Watch, 3:00 a.m. to 6:00 a.m.)" (Mark 13: 35).

"Lest coming suddenly he find you sleeping and what I say unto you I say unto all, 'Watch'" (Mark 15:36-37).

Intercessors pour out rivers of intercession during the night watches! Each watch has strategic approaches for effective prayer.

FIRST WATCH OF NIGHT

The watch lasts from 6:00 p.m. to 9:00 p.m. The Jewish day begins during this watch. Jesus healed many sick people during this watch (Mark 1:32). It is a time for quiet meditation, to study and reflect on God's Word. During the evening, Isaac went to meditate as he longed for a true wife. As he lifted his eyes, he saw camels coming, bringing his future wife (Genesis 24:63-67). Camels signify provisions; when a company of camels came to a region, they brought supplies and riches. This is a watch to pray for your financial concerns, asking God to provide the provisions you need. Remember that the Lord's Prayer tells us to pray that God will give us our daily bread.

THE SECOND WATCH OF THE NIGHT

The hours for this watch are from 9:00 p.m. to midnight. Special divine favor is associated with this watch. The Egyptians were so desperate for the children of Israel to leave that they gave away their riches. The people of Egypt suffered greatly from the judgment plagues, and the plague of the death of the first-born sons caused much distress among the Egyptians. This may have been the watch time that they departed because it was before the midnight hour. For it was at midnight that the death of the first-born sons of the Egyptians occurred. This plague of death was a judgment upon the nation.

And the Lord said unto Moses, Yet will I bring one more plague upon Pharoah, and upon Egypt; afterward he will let you go hence: when he shall let you go, he shall surely thrust you out hence altogether. Speak now in the ears of the people, and let every man borrow of his neighbor, and every woman of her neighbor, jewels of silver, and jewels of gold. And the Lord gave the people FAVOR in the sight of the Egyptians, Moreover the Man Moses was very great in the land of Egypt, in the sight of Pharaoh's servants, and in the sight of the people. (Exodus 11:1-3 KJV)

Pray for favor and provisions during this watch!

THE THIRD WATCH OF THE NIGHT

The third watch of the night includes the hours from midnight until 3:00 a.m. King David was a man of prayer, and he spoke about this watch.

"At midnight I will rise to give thanks unto you because of your righteous judgments" (Psalm 119:62).

King David was not the only one to praise the Lord at midnight. Paul and Silas praised the Lord from a prison cell. They were placed in prison by evil men who accused them falsely. Their feet were in stocks. They were bound. They suffered great discomfort. Yet, during the third watch of the night, they praised the Lord! Their praises and prayers rose into the spiritual atmosphere. They opened the doors of heaven with a river of prayer.

"Then suddenly an earthquake occurred. The force of the earthquake was so great that it opened the prison doors and loosed the bands on all the prisoners!" (Acts 16:25-34).

Deliverance from the chains of evil is the theme of this prayer watch. This is an ideal time to pray for those who are in bondage and afflicted.

Others were also released at midnight. God released the people of Israel from the cruel bondage inflicted upon them by the Egyptians. At midnight the Lord smote all the first-born in the land of Egypt (Exodus 12:29).

"And he (Pharoah) called for Moses and Aaron by night, and said, Rise up and get you forth from among my people, both you and the children of Israel; and go, serve the Lord, as you have said" (Exodus 12:31).

THE FOURTH WATCH OF THE NIGHT

The traditional hours for this watch are 3:00 a.m. to 6:00 a.m. Several exciting events occurred during this watch. Jesus came walking on the water toward the disciples' boat during the fourth watch (Matthew 14:25 KJV).

"And he (Jesus) saw them toiling in the rowing; for the wind was contrary unto them: and about the fourth watch of the night he came unto them, walking upon the sea, and would have passed by them" (Mark 6:48).

One important message is do not let Jesus pass you by.

Be awake and alert on your watch! Another great victory happened during the morning watch. The Lord appeared in a pillar of fire and of a cloud and looked down upon the Egyptians. He overthrew their forces. This was the army that pursued Moses and the children of Israel when they departed from Egypt!

> *So it happened at the early morning watch (before dawn), that the Lord looked down upon the army of the Egyptians through the pillar of fire and cloud and put them in a state of confusion. He made their chariot wheels hard to turn, and the chariots difficult to drive; so the Egyptians said, "Let us flee from Israel, for the Lord is fighting for them against the Egyptians"* (Exodus 14:24-25 The Amplified Study Bible)

The message for those who pray during the morning watch is

"God will fight for you." You will not be alone in your battles; God will assist you and grant you a great victory. Jesus Himself also prayed during the morning watch.

"And in the morning, rising up a great while before day, he (Jesus) went out, and departed into a solitary place, and prayed" (Mark 1:35 KJV).

RELEASE A RIVER OF FRESH INCENSE

It was the duty of the priest to offer a sacrifice of sweet incense during the morning watch.

"And Aaron (the Priest) shall burn thereon sweet incense every morning: when he dresses the lamps, he shall burn incense upon it" (Exodus 30:7 KJV).

The events of your day can go very well if you release a river of fresh incense during the morning watch!

MY PRAYER EVERY MORNING

This is a scripture that I pray most every morning. It is a prayer for instruction, and a prayer for my mouth to speak life to others!

"The Lord has given me the tongue of the learned, that I should know how to speak a word in season to him that is weary, he wakes my ear to hear as the learned. The Lord God has opened my ear, and I was not rebellious, neither turned away back" (Isaiah 50:4-5).

Will you release a river of sweet intercession during the night watches? If you do, you will experience many victories!

CHAPTER 9

ANGELS BY THE RIVERS

I have had some extraordinary experiences along the banks of rivers. When I was a teenager, I loved to go fly fishing with my dad. He was an expert fly fisherman who knew the types of flies the fish were feeding on and even tied his own flies. I still remember the names of some of the most effective ones: the Royal Coachman, the Gnat, the Woolly Bugger, and the Gray Wolf.

One evening, about thirty minutes before dark, we stood along the bank of a river in Sugar Grove, Virginia. It was a glorious sight to behold. The moon shone upon the water and a few stars added to the beauty. Rainbow trout were jumping high out of the water to capture flies with their mouths, and small patches of fog hung over the river. A peaceful feeling engulfed me, and at that moment, I was sure that there was a God. Through nature, God had revealed Himself to me.

"The heavens declare the glory of God; and the firmament shows his handiwork. Day unto day utters speech, and night unto night shows knowledge" (Psalm 19:1-2 KJV).

TRAUMA TERMINATED ON THE BANKS OF THE HOLSTON RIVER

Here, we were praying on the banks of the Holston River. I was a student at Emory & Henry College in Emory, Virginia. I was on a search for God's presence and longed to be filled with His Spirit.

"As the hart pants after the water brooks, so pants my soul after you, O God. My soul thirsts for God, for the living God: when shall I come and appear before God" (Psalm 42:1-2).

The pastor and the prayer team were praying for me. I had experienced a traumatic event as a senior in high school. It weighed heavily on my mind. I did not understand why it happened to me. I needed God to heal the memories that caused pain. As they prayed, the place lit up with the most brilliant light. I saw Jesus standing over me when that event happened. A cloud surrounded Jesus as He stood over me. He reminded me that I did not suffer true physical harm. Heaven alerted me to run as fast as I could, and I ran. But the terror of the thing still haunted me. Then suddenly, all fear left and the emotional pain left me. I could still remember the event, but there was no pain. A weight was lifted off my mind and my emotions. Peace filled that void, and faith replaced fear. I was able to forgive. My freedom came at the banks of a river!

AT THE POOL OF BETHESDA

A well-known angel came to the Pool of Bethesda. Interestingly, the name Bethesda refers to the "House of Mercy," where mercy would be imparted to those who could enter the pool first. The pool was surrounded by people with various infirmities, such as the lame and those suffering from great afflictions. Some people held onto their crutches as they intently watched the water in the pool. When Jesus arrived, many were still fixated on the pool, eagerly waiting for an angel to come and stir the waters (John 5:4). They knew that an angel would come during certain seasons and "trouble" the water (John 5:4). The people could see the waters rising up and bubbling. The very first person to enter the water after the angel stirred it would be healed. Jesus approached the man who had been afflicted for thirty-eight years and engaged him in a conversation. The man had been focused on the water for so long, closely watching for even the slightest movement.

"Sir, I have no man, when the water is troubled, to put me into the pool: but while I am coming, another (person) steps down before me" (John 5:7).

Maybe the man was hoping that Jesus would help him get into the pool before anyone else. But Jesus had a message for him: "The angel may be used to bring healing, but I am the source of life and healing!"

"Rise take up your bed, and walk" (John 5:8).

Immediately, healing came! The man picked up his bed and walked! He had longed to walk for many years. Now he was walking!

BY THE RIVER OF CHEBAR

It was by the river of Chebar that the heavens opened and visions of God were seen by Ezekiel. Ezekiel was a prophet, and he was also from a family of priests. He was carried away to Babylon as a captive in 597 B.C., along with the children of Israel. He ministered to the captives who lived by the river of Chebar at Tel Ahib. At the river, Ezekiel experienced a supernatural encounter. *"The word of the Lord came expressly unto Ezekiel the priest, the son of Buzi, in the land of the Chaldeans by the river of Chebar; and the hand of the Lord was there upon him"* (Ezekiel 1:3). He saw spiritual beings known as cherubim, who have the duty of guarding God's throne.

106

This glorious vision showed the cherubim supporting the throne as they burst out of a whirlwind. They were bright and displayed the color of amber. It looked like they had just come out of the midst of a fire (Ezekiel 1:4). These visions provided comfort and reassurance, conveying the message that God has not abandoned His people and still reigns upon His throne. There were four cherubim, each with four faces— the face of a man, the face of a lion, the face of an ox, and the face of an eagle (Ezekiel 1:10). They had wings, and the hands of a man were under their wings on all four sides (Ezekiel 1:6-10). Their wings were joined to each other and they moved straight forward. Another interesting aspect of the vision was the wheel in the middle of a wheel. These wheels allowed them to move in any direction. The wheels touched the earth but still reached heaven (Ezekiel 1:16). The wheels symbolized that God was still working on the earth.

"The appearance of the wheels and their work was like unto the color of beryl: and they four had one likeness: and their appearance and their work was as it were a wheel in the middle of a wheel" (Ezekiel 1:16).

They looked like burning coals as they darted about.

GOD IS STILL ON HIS THRONE

This vision brought comfort to the captives. As mentioned, the wheels suggested that God was still working on the earth. Nothing could stop these wheels. Likewise, nothing can stop God's work on the earth! The final part of the vision was a view of God's throne. Despite the captivity, God was still on His throne. And He still reigned in heaven and earth!

And I saw as the color of amber, as the appearance of fire round about within it, from the appearance of his loins even upward, and from the appearance of his loins even downward, I saw as it were the appearance of fire, and it had brightness round about.

As the appearance of the bow that is in the cloud in the day of rain, so was the appearance of the brightness round about. This was the appearance of the likeness of the glory of the Lord. And when I saw it, I fell upon my face, and I heard a voice of one that spoke. (Ezekiel 1:27-28)

This vision by the river of Chebar reassured Ezekiel that God is all-powerful and all-knowing!

BY THE RIVER HIDDEKEL

A final vision relating to the future of the nation of Israel was given to Daniel on the banks of the great river, Hiddekel. The Hiddekel was famous and held historical significance as one of the rivers of the Garden of Eden (Genesis 2:1-4). It was said to flow east to Assyria and is usually identified with the Tigris River, known for its rapid flow of water.

This vision came after Daniel had spent three weeks fasting, consuming no pleasant bread, meat, or wine, and not anointing himself with oil (Daniel 10:3). Daniel states that he was in a period of mourning, which appears to have occurred during Passover and the Feast of Unleavened Bread. During this time, he looked up and saw a spiritual being that appeared to be a mighty angel. The angel was clothed in linen, and his loins were covered with fine gold.

"His body also was like the beryl, and his face as the appearance of lightning, and his eyes as lamps of fire, and his arms and his feet like in color to polished brass, and the voice of his words like the voice of thunder" (Daniel 10:5-6).

His appearance and the sound of his voice suggested that he may have been an angel of war. Daniel became very weak when he saw this angel. He said that no strength remained in him (Daniel 10:8). He was lying on his face in a deep sleep (Daniel 10:9-10).

The angel touched Daniel, helping him rise to his knees and support himself upon the palms of his hands.

FROM THE FIRST DAY

The angel assured Daniel that from the first day he prayed and sought God, his prayer was heard (Daniel 10:12). Intercessors should be encouraged to know that on the very first day they began to pray over a matter, their prayers are heard by heaven (Daniel 10:12). Sometimes, delay of answers occurs when we pray. A heavenly explanation is given for times of delay – a heavenly war was being fought over nations, causing the delay. This evidence confirms that territorial spirits are attempting to rule over regions and even nations. This is why our prayers are so important. Like Daniel, we can pray for angels to fight for our cities, our towns, and our regions. We can also pray for angels to be released to defend our nation. The angel tells Daniel that he was delayed by the heavenly warfare.

"Then said he unto me, Fear not, Daniel: for from the first day that you did set thine heart to understand, and to chasten thyself before thy God, thy words were heard, and I am come for thy words" (Daniel 10:12).

Angels come when you release prayers, especially when those prayers declare the Scriptures (Psalm 103:20). Angels can come for your children, your family, your job situation, and even your finances. They are waiting for you to release scriptural prayers. When these types of prayers are released into the atmosphere, angels are activated.

HEAVENLY WARFARE ALONG THE RIVER

Next, the angel describes the warfare in the heavenlies, just above Daniel and the nation. So often, we are accustomed to witnessing physical warfare. Army tanks, helicopters, drones, and bombs are some of the weapons visible to the physical eye. However, if we could look up into the heavens, we would see spiritual beings engaged in battles over regions. Daniel's prayers helped bring victory in these spiritual battles, and your prayers will do the same! The angel speaks of a spiritual being over the kingdom of Persia.

"But the prince of the kingdom of Persia withstood me one and twenty days: but, lo, Michael one of the chief princes, came to help me; and I remained there with the kings of Persia" (Daniel 10: 13).

Michael would bring great help. He is portrayed as an angel

110

who is mighty in warfare. He was known to possess supernatural strength and speed. He is also called the "Great Prince," which stands for the nation of Israel (Daniel 12:1).

ANOTHER ANGEL AND ANOTHER NATION

The angel informed Daniel that as soon as he finished his assignment of giving him instructions, he would return to the battle, and another demonic spirit would go to another nation for war.

"Then said he, 'Knowest thou wherefore I come unto thee? and now I will return to fight with the prince of Persia: and when I am gone forth, lo, the prince of Grecia shall come'" (Daniel 10:20).

WHO ARE THESE PRINCES?

Both the Prince of Grecia and the Prince of Persia were demons who worked through these nations to oppose God's people.

ALONG THE BANKS OF THE RIVER

Daniel discovered that along the banks of the river, both angels and demonic spirits could be found. While the banks of the river could be places of great spiritual experiences, they could also be places of heavenly warfare!

A PRAYER MEETING BY THE RIVER

Significant spiritual events occurred by riverbanks. One major experience along the banks of a river occurred when Paul attended a prayer meeting. Both Paul and Silas had traveled to the city of Philippi, a major city in the district of Macedonia. This region was under Roman rule (Acts 16:12). Paul attended a prayer meeting by a riverbank. At this prayer meeting, he met key people who would assist him.

"And on the Sabbath day we went outside the city gate to the bank of the (Gangites) river, where we thought there would be a place of prayer, and we sat down and began speaking to the women who had come there" (Acts 16:13 The Amplified Study Bible).

When Paul and Silas prayed, their prayers were filled with promises from the Scriptures. People were healed and delivered from demons when they prayed! And when God's Word is released in prayers, angels stand ready for action.

"Bless the Lord, you His angels, You mighty ones who do His commandments, Obeying the voice of His word!" (Psalm 103:20 The Amplified Study Bible).

PEOPLE OF PRAYER AND PEOPLE OF THE OCCULT

A famous woman named Lydia met Paul at the prayer meeting by the riverbank. She was a successful businesswoman. This woman and her household accepted the gospel message preached by Paul. She also invited Paul and Silas to stay in her house during their mission in Thyatira. She provided great hospitality. However, a demonic spirit also hung around the riverbank. It was known as the spirit of divination. It brought great distress to Paul and Silas.

"And it came to pass, as we went to prayer, a certain damsel possessed with a spirit of divination met us, which brought her masters much gain by soothsaying" (Acts 16:16).

Everywhere that Paul and Silas went, she followed. She cried out, *"These men are the servants of the most-high God. which show unto us the way of salvation"* (Acts 16:17).

Can you imagine someone yelling over you? Paul and Silas found it difficult to preach the gospel because this spirit created great distractions. For many days, this spirit possessed the girl and grieved Paul and Silas (Acts 16:18). Finally, Paul would not tolerate the evil spirit any longer. He turned and spoke to the spirit, commanding it to leave the girl in the name of Jesus Christ. That same hour, the spirit came out of the girl. She was free from the spirit of divination (Acts 16:18). Paul and Silas defeated demonic spirits along the banks of a river, where prayer meetings were held!

BAPTIZED AT THE JORDAN RIVER

Perhaps one of the most significant experiences to occur at a river was the baptism of Jesus. Jesus asked John the Baptist to baptize Him. With a humble attitude, John told Jesus that He was the one who should be doing the baptism and that he should be baptized by Him (Matthew 3:14-15). What a glorious scene the disciples beheld when Jesus came up from the water.

"And Jesus when he was baptized, went up straightway out of

the water: and lo, the heavens were opened unto him, and he saw the Spirit of God descending like a dove, and lightning upon him" (Matthew 3:16).

What a privilege to see the heavens open! Next, a dove came from heaven and landed upon Jesus. The dove was a symbol of innocence and purity. Also, the dove was a symbolic representation of the Holy Spirit. And there was more. A voice sounded from heaven.

"And lo a voice from heaven, saying, 'This is my beloved Son, in whom I am well pleased'" (Matthew 3:17).

There could be no doubt that Jesus was sent by God!

TIME TO COME TO THE RIVER

The river is waiting for us! For at the river, we can experience an outpouring of God's Spirit. Like the woman at the well, we can encounter the One who gives everlasting water. Many people have become weary. Others have faced disappointments. A refreshing of God's presence is the answer.

"But whosoever drinks the water that I shall give him shall never thirst; but the water that I shall give him shall be in him a well of water springing up into everlasting life" (John 4:14).

CHAPTER 10

ARE YOU WINNING OR LOSING THE BATTLE?

I recall a time in my life when I faced great challenges. Every effort to achieve victory was unsuccessful. Even my determination to pray fell short. Day after day, there was no good news. It even seemed that things were getting worse.

REEVALUATE

If I continued to push in these efforts, failure would surely come, and the lives of people depended on me to succeed. So, I returned to the River of Knowledge. This heavenly view of three spiritual rivers turned my efforts from failure to success! The River of Knowledge branches off from the River of Life. I asked for wisdom to turn from failure to victory.

"If any of you lacks wisdom (to guide him through a decision or circumstance), he is to ask of (our benevolent God, who gives to everyone generously and without rebuke or blame, and it will be given him" (James 1:5 The Amplified Study Bible).

Praying in the fourth watch of the night for a few weeks was the answer that I received. And the very first time that I prayed on this watch, answers came quickly. Within a couple of weeks, victories were achieved!

NOT THE ONLY ONE

I am not the only one who needs knowledge and understanding. I am not the only one who needs to reevaluate situations. There was a time when seven of Jesus' disciples went on a fishing trip. It was only natural for them to return to their original vocation before meeting Jesus. They had just witnessed Jesus' cruel death and seen Him come back in a resur-

118

rected body. They had also heard Him say that He would return to heaven. They had heard Jesus preach and seen Him perform marvelous miracles. Yet, they were uncertain about the direction of their lives. Maybe a fishing trip would help them both financially and emotionally. Therefore, they went to the Sea of Tiberias and sailed approximately 134 yards from shore.

Jesus appeared on the shore in the morning, ready to help them reevaluate their situation. This was the third time that Jesus showed Himself to the majority of the apostles and the seventh appearance since His resurrection. He had spent a lot of time with them and had great plans for their lives. They would be instrumental in forming the Christian church and spreading the gospel throughout the world. When the disciples saw Jesus standing on the shore, they did not recognize that it was Him (John 21:4). He asked them if they had caught any fish, essentially asking if their fishing trip had been successful. Their answer to Jesus was no. They had fished all night but caught nothing. Next, Jesus gave them instructions.

"And he said unto them, Cast the net on the right side of the ship, (star-board) and you shall find some. So, they cast (the net), and they were not able to haul it in because of the great catch of fish" (John 21:6 The Amplified Study Bible).

UNDERSTAND THE MESSAGE

If they kept fishing on the left side of the boat, they would fail. They wouldn't catch any fish, and they would suffer financial loss and physical exhaustion. Without Jesus (the River of Life), they would struggle and come back home with no fish and no money. When Peter heard that it was Jesus standing on the shore and talking to them, he jumped from the boat and swam to Him. Jesus told Peter to bring some of the fish they had caught. It was time for breakfast! Now, Peter saw the miracle that had just happened. He informed Jesus that there were 153 large fish in the net. It was a miracle that it didn't break. It was a miraculous catch of fish. Jesus showed that the Lord could supply every need the disciples would face. They could become ministers of the gospel with the assurance that the Lord could and would take care of their needs.

ONE HUNDRED AND FIFTY-THREE FISH

This number of fish has intrigued me. Upon further study, I realized that it was not merely the actual number of fish, but rather the extraordinary catch itself. This was not a typical catch for fishermen during the time of the disciples, but rather a miraculous one. The disciples had just witnessed a miracle! This extraordinary event strengthened their faith in Jesus and in His ability to provide.

DO YOU NEED DIRECTION FOR YOUR LIFE?

If things seem unclear to you at this point in your life, look to the River of Life. Are you confused about some situations? If so, look to the River of Life. Are you uncertain as to how to proceed? Ask for wisdom and look to the River of Knowledge! Peter still needed assurance. The amazing catch of fish did inspire him, and he truly wanted to follow the plan that Jesus had for his life. But one question hung over his head. Three times he had denied Jesus. Yes, while Jesus was suffering on the cross, Peter denied Him. He had been overcome by fear. He probably did not feel worthy to spread the gospel to the world.

GOD HAS A PLAN

God has plans for your life, and the best thing you can do is to pursue them. He proved to Peter that when He has a plan, He also makes provision. If you find yourself losing many spiritual battles, take a moment to reevaluate your life. It may be that you are not following God's best plans for you and your family.

DO YOU LOVE ME?

Three times on the shore of the Sea of Tiberias, Jesus asked Peter the same question. Three times, Peter denied Jesus when he was afflicted on the cross.

> *So when they had finished breakfast, Jesus said to Simon Peter, "Simon, son of John, do you love Me more that these (others do---with total commitment and devotion)?" He said to Him, "Yes, Lord: you know that I love You (with a deep, personal affection, for a close friend)." Jesus said to him, "Feed my lambs.*
> (John 21:15 The Amplified Study Bible)

Love is a verb in this request of Jesus. If you love Me, "Feed my lambs." Do not just say you love Me; do the work of the gospel. Feed God's people by teaching them the Scriptures. Feed His people by praying for them to be healed. Feed His

121

people by assisting with their needs.

A RIVER OF KNOWLEDGE FOR YOU

Victories are coming to you. You no longer have to suffer losses. Reevaluate your life and ask for wisdom. Come to the River of Knowledge (Jesus) and follow God's plan for your life. Any other plan will result in struggle, pain, loss, and disappointment.

RIGHT SOURCE EQUALS RIGHT RESULTS

The heavenly view that I saw during a time of prayer can be summarized as follows. Out of a heart flowed three rivers. There was a main river, known as the "River of Life." One river branched out from the main river. The name of this river was the "River of Knowledge." Another river branched out from the other side of the main river. The name of this river was the "River of Healing." These rivers brought great victories to the regions that they flowed through.

CONNECTIONS

An electrician certainly knows the importance of making the right connections. Certain wires are designed to fit into designated conduits so that they can function properly and provide safety. On the other hand, if wires are connected to the wrong places, they can explode and cause significant harm. How does this apply to us? We need to connect with the correct river, just like the woman at the well (John 4:15). Additionally, we must be aware of the source of that river. With great desire, she asked Jesus for this water.

"The woman said to Him, "Sir, give me this water, so that I will not get thirsty nor (have to continually) come all the way here to draw" (John 4:15).

The source is the first part of the heavenly view.

FROM THE THRONE OF GOD

A spring of water flows from underground. A spring is a natural place where water flows out of the ground. This underground water may start as a trickle and then suddenly become a large flow of water. One famous spring that we used to visit is called Shatley Springs. My dad loved telling us about the healing properties of Shatley Springs, which is located at 407 Shatley Springs Road, Crumbler, N.C. (near Sparta). In addition to the healing waters, there is a famous restaurant that serves delicious home-cooked meals. Some people come for the food, while others come for the spring water. People bring empty jugs and fill them with the water from the spring. I remember seeing people lining up and waiting for their turn to gather water in their jugs.

The history of the springs tells the story of a man named Martin Shatley. On a summer day in 1890, he stumbled upon these springs. He dipped his hands and face in the water. Just a few hours later, he realized that he was healed of a crippling skin disease that had plagued him for many years. The news of these springs quickly spread, and soon many people came to visit these healing waters!

WATER FLOWED FROM THE TEMPLE

Ezekiel was given a vision of water flowing from the temple

(Ezekiel 47:1). His guide led him to the river. At first, they waded in the river up to their ankles. Then they continued in the river to a knee-deep level. Finally, they swam in the river. Everywhere the river flowed, everything lived! (Ezekiel 47:9). But of great importance was the fact that the river flowed from underneath the temple.

> *Then he (my guide) brought me back to the door of the house (the temple of the Lord): and behold, water was flowing from under the threshold of the of the house (temple) toward the east. And the water was flowing down from under, from the right side of the house, from the south of the altar. Then he brought me out by way of the north gate and led me around on the outside to the outer gate by the way of the gate that faces east. And behold, water was spurting out from the south side (of the gate).*
> (Ezekiel 47:1-2 The Amplified Study Bible)

Another reference to this river shows it flowing from the throne of God.

"Then the angel showed me a river of the water of life, clear as crystal, flowing from the throne of God, and of the Lamb (Christ)" (Revelation 22:1 The Amplified Study Bible).

THE SECOND PART OF THE HEAVENLY SIGHT

I took karate classes and learned about the importance of proper breathing. Deep breaths, originating from the belly, are produced. Next, the student is instructed to exhale slowly, ensuring that the breath is released through the mouth, not the nose. After a slow exhalation, the student then inhales slowly, directing the inhalation down toward the belly. Often, the student will place her hands on her own belly to feel the flow of exhalation and inhalation. This technique is known as Ki breathing and it aids in relaxation and focus. Students must dedicate ample time to practicing this type of breathing before they can progress to other skills. It is important to note that this breathing technique can be taught without affiliating with any particular religion. A scripture that reminds me of this concept is:

> *Now on the last and most important day of the feast, Jesus stood and called out (in a loud voice), If anyone is thirsty, let him come to Me and drink. He who believes in Me (who adheres to, trusts in, and relies on Me), as the Scripture has said, "From his innermost being will flow continually rivers of living water.* (John 7: 38 The Amplified Study Bible)

An underground spring is released in prayer to produce mighty victories!

FROM THE HEART

From the belly, this powerful expression in the form of prayer flows toward the heart. Prayer does not create the river; the River of Life is its source! When we pray, it flows to us and through us, having a mighty impact and a multiplying effect. The value of a heartfelt prayer cannot be underestimated.

"The heartfelt and consistent prayer of a righteous man (believer) can accomplish much (when put into action and made effective by God --- it is dynamic and can have tremendous power)" (James 5: 16 The Amplified Study Bible).

The person who prepares his heart to receive God's Word will be noticed.

My son, pay attention to my words and be willing to learn; Open your ears to my sayings. Do not let them escape from your sight: Keep them in the center of your heart, For they are life to those who find them, And healing and health to all their flesh, Watch over your heart with all diligence, For from it flow the springs of life. (Proverbs 4:20-24 The Amplified Study Bible)

FINALLY! A BREAKTHROUGH WITH VICTORY

I saw three rivers flowing from the heart. The main river had two branches. Like arrows from skilled warriors, prayers were released to their targets. Breakthroughs began to happen. People rejoiced. Lost individuals came back home. Many who were afflicted in soul and body were healed. Financial resources were released for those who prayed with zeal. People who had lost hope were encouraged. These prayers released mighty declarations of the Scriptures. God's Word was prayed with skill by seasoned warriors!

"For with God nothing (is or ever) shall be impossible" (Luke 1:37 The Amplified Study Bible).

ABOUT THE AUTHOR

Mary Donna Hankla is an intercessor who strongly believes that God is a waymaker. She believes in the power of effective prayers to release Heaven's power into present situations. "Thus says the LORD, which makes a way in the sea, and a path in the mighty waters" (Isaiah 43:16). Mary has faced challenging situations and difficult people, but she has also witnessed the victories that God has brought. She greatly appreciates her husband and son, Kenny and Chris Hankla, who provide vital support for her ministry.

For over 22 years, Donna has been an active minister with the International Pentecostal Holiness Church (IPHC) and is also an ordained minister. She serves in the Appalachian Conference as a pastor and director of the WIN prayer program (World-Wide Intercessory Network). She has led many prayer watches, including Night-Watch, 24-Hour Prayer Watch, and 21-Day Daniel Fast, for the church and conference. Donna has participated in the National Day of Prayer in Washington, D.C., for 15 years, as well as prayer events sponsored by the Capitol Hill Prayer Partners, led by Sara Ballenger, and Women's Aglow. She has also led prayer walks to key regions such as Mount Mitchell in North Carolina. Since 2007, Donna has been a pastor at the Big Four Church in Kimball, WV. Currently, she works with a community action group that assists pregnant mothers and children up to the age of three.

Mary Donna Hankla can be followed using the QR codes on the back of this book.